A GIFT FOR:

Withdrawn from Collection

PRESENTED BY:

Withdrawn from Collection

WHAT IF HUMANS WERE LIKE ANIMALS?

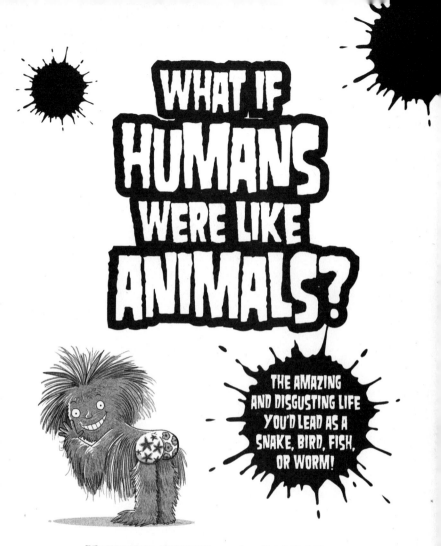

THE AMAZING AND DISGUSTING LIFE YOU'D LEAD AS A SNAKE, BIRD, FISH, OR WORM!

MARIANNE TAYLOR AND LAUREN TAYLOR

Reader's Digest

The Reader's Digest Association, Inc.

New York, NY/Montreal

A READER'S DIGEST BOOK

Text and illustrations copyright © Buster Books 2013

Reader's Digest is a registered trademark of
The Reader's Digest Association, Inc.

First published in Great Britain in 2013 by Buster Books, an imprint of Michael
O'Mara Books Limited, 9 Lion Yard, Tremadoc Road, London SW4 7NQ

Concept and illustration by Paul Moran

Additional illustration details from www.shutterstock.com

Library of Congress Cataloging in Publication Data is available upon request.

ISBN 978-1-62145-030-6

We are committed to both the quality of our products
and the service we provide to our customers.
We value your comments, so please feel free to contact us.

The Reader's Digest Association, Inc.
Adult Trade Publishing
44 South Broadway
White Plains, NY 10601

For more Reader's Digest products and information, visit our website:
www.rd.com (in the United States)
www.readersdigest.ca (in Canada)

Printed in the United States of America

1 3 5 7 9 10 8 6 4 2

CONTENTS

What If . . .

CONTENTS

. . . HUMANS WERE LIKE ANIMALS?

Do your parents ever complain that you're behaving like an animal? They usually mean that you are being messy or eating with your mouth open, but what if humans really were like animals?

Sometimes rats eat some of their own young to make sure that only the healthiest babies survive. If humans did this, you'd have to be careful not to annoy your dad! But it's not all bad—there are plenty of amazing things you could do if you were like an animal. Before you turn the page to find out more, check out the ratings below to tell the freaky from the fearsome and the useful from the yucky.

 Beware a score of five—these creepy creatures are almost too scary to read about.

 For the smarty pants of the animal world, a high score will leave you feeling dumbfounded.

 A high score will make you wish for this fantastic animal feature, but a low score will have you thankful you're a human.

 Encounter a score of five and you might have trouble keeping down your lunch.

. . . YOU HAD EYES ON YOUR HANDS?

If you are lucky, you have two eyes, which your mom probably tells you are beautiful. But what if you had eight eyes like a spider, or even a hundred like a scallop? Your mom would still love you, but other people might stare.

Handy Eyes

What if you had eyes on the ends of your arms like a starfish? Sure, it might be pretty gross to have eyeballs sticking out of the palms of your hands, but think how easily you could check around corners or read other people's magazines at the bus stop. You could even read two magazines at the same time, if you felt like it.

One Hundred Peepers

Scallops are snail-like sea creatures. Some of them have a hundred eyes that they use to spot predators. If you had a hundred eyes, you could watch TV, read this book, check your e-mail, stare out the window, and watch your own back— all at the same time.

A fly has two eyes, but each contains thousands of lenses. That would look kind of creepy . . .

. . . YOUR EYEBALLS GREW HAIR?

Hairy Eyeballs

Honeybees have hairy eyeballs, which help them figure out which way the wind is blowing. Knowing wind speed and direction is pretty important if you plan to fly. You wouldn't want to crash and burn before you got to that sunflower you've been eyeing all day. The hairs also help bees carry pollen and nectar from one place to another.

Half Asleep

A dolphin always sleeps with one eye open. When feeling sleepy, it turns on its side and floats on the surface of the ocean. It closes the eye that's facing the sky, but the eye in the water stays open—keeping it in a semiawake state that allows it to continue breathing and watch out for predators.

A Real Eyeful

Here are some more eye-opening animal facts:

- An ostrich's eye weighs more than its brain.

- Some squid have eyes bigger than dinner plates.

- Camels have three eyelids to protect their eyes from the blowing sand in the desert.

- Owls can't move their eyes but follow their prey by moving their necks, which can rotate an amazing 270°, or three-fourths of the way around.

...YOUR EYES COULD SQUIRT BLOOD?

Could your eyes ever be gruesome enough to scare someone silly? It would be a cool trick if they could—though your victims might not agree. Here is an eye-popping animal trait you might find useful . . .

Bursting Blood

A horned lizard can burst the blood vessels in its eyes, and shoot a stream of blood a distance of up to five feet (one and a half meters). Imagine trick-or-treating—you are dressed in your creepiest costume, your neighbor opens the door, you take aim and—SQUIRT—you spray. Just make sure you get your hands on the sweets first, as people might not feel very generous when they're covered in blood.

SCARY 5 SCORE

... YOUR EYES WERE ON ONE SIDE OF YOUR HEAD?

Eyes are always very useful, no matter where they are on an animal's body. Your eyes are carefully positioned on your face so that you can see lots of things around you.

Eyes on the Side
A flatfish has both eyes on one side of its head, so it can hide on the ocean floor and still see. Great for a flatfish, but if you only had eyes on one side of your head, it would be very easy for a thief to steal your wallet.

Fascinating, Freaky Fact
Hippos and crocodiles have eyes on top of their heads, so they can see above the water while hiding in it. Very useful for games of hide-and-seek.

. . . YOUR EARS WERE BIGGER THAN YOUR HEAD?

Your ears aren't just for hearing. You probably think they are also useful for supporting your headphones and holding up your sunglasses. But what if they had more interesting functions? Giant ears might look ridiculous, but they would keep you chilled in the heat of the sun.

Cooling Off

It can be scorching hot in Africa, where some types of elephant live. One way elephants deal with the heat is by flapping their large ears to keep cool. So forget an electric fan—just wiggle your ears.

But what happens when your enormous ears get in the way? No problem . . . just fold them up like the long-eared bat when you aren't using them.

HOW HANDY 3

Fascinating, Freaky Fact
Seals can close their ears to keep water out when they are swimming. You could ditch your earplugs when diving for tasty fishy treats.

Did You Catch That?
Would you like to know when people are talking about you? All you'd need are ears twice as long as your head, like a jackrabbit's, and you would be able to hear every word. Huge ears might be a bit *ear*-ritating, but it's a small price to pay for supersonic hearing.

. . . YOUR MOUTH WERE ON YOUR STOMACH?

What if your mouth wasn't on your face? What if it were big enough for you to stuff in all your favorite foods at once?

A Feast Fit for a Starfish

If your mouth were where a starfish's mouth is, it'd be right in the middle of your body—on your stomach. You could munch away on a midnight feast while dozing off. Here's how:

1. Lean on a pile of pillows so that you are sitting up.

2. Lay out your favorite snacks nearby, and make sure your stomach mouth has easy access to them.

3. Now sleep tight and let your stomach bite. You might want to wear earplugs in case the slurping noises get too loud.

ROTTEN
3
RATING

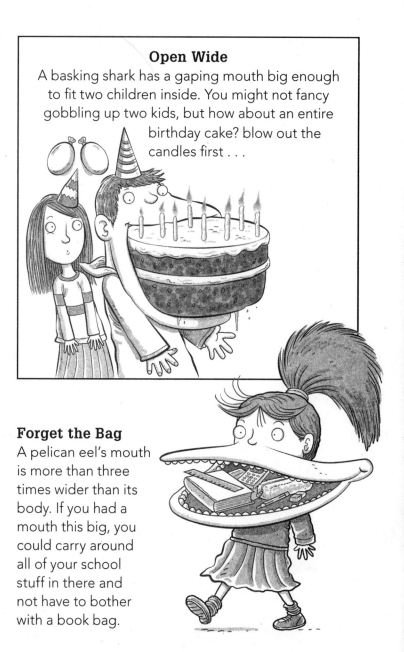

Open Wide

A basking shark has a gaping mouth big enough to fit two children inside. You might not fancy gobbling up two kids, but how about an entire birthday cake? blow out the candles first . . .

Forget the Bag

A pelican eel's mouth is more than three times wider than its body. If you had a mouth this big, you could carry around all of your school stuff in there and not have to bother with a book bag.

. . . YOU NEVER HAD TO BRUSH YOUR TEETH?

From having giant teeth that grow past your chin to never having to brush your teeth, seriously strange gnashers come in handy for all sorts of reasons.

Great Pearly Whites

Here are some excellent reasons to have shark teeth:

- If you lose any teeth, don't worry—they will be replaced by a brand-new set! You could have all of the sweets and fizzy drinks you like and never have to brush your teeth.

- No dentist will want to come near you, as your pearly whites would be super sharp.

- Whenever you want to frighten anyone, just open wide.

A Toothy Grin

A babirusa pig's upper teeth grow up instead of down, bursting right out of its face. If your teeth grew this way, you'd have a truly spectacular smile.

Say Cheese!

Saber-toothed cats, now extinct, had enormous fangs that grew well below their chins. Would you have liked these on school picture day?

. . . YOU COULD TASTE WITH YOUR FEET?

Do you love food? If the answer is yes, imagine how cool it would be to taste or smell it with other parts of your body—or even your whole body.

What a Feat!

What if you could taste with your feet like a butterfly? You could be chewing gum while tasting cake batter at the same time. The only problem is, would you really want to eat food that you'd walked all over? If you serve the cake to your friends, just make sure you don't tell them that your stinky feet have been in it.

ROTTEN 3 RATING

Tasty Bath

Catfish can smell and taste with their whole bodies. Just imagine—you could submerge yourself in a giant glass of cool lemonade on a hot day. Or if you're crazy about chocolate, you could have your morning bath in warm chocolate sauce every day. Delicious!

Smell It with Flowers

A snake smells the air with its tongue—the forked tip helps it figure out where a smell is coming from. If this were the way your mom smelled, she'd wave her tongue around when you brought her flowers on Mother's Day.

. . . YOU HAD CRAZY HAIR?

Most people have hair on their heads, and some people have very long hair. But what if you were covered in long hair from head to toe?

Dreadful Locks

The Komondor is a dog breed that has floor-length dreadlocks all over its body. With hair like this, you might be mistaken for a mop.

Bottoms Up!

Hair is useful stuff—it can even keep you warm in cold weather, which would come in handy if you didn't wear clothes, like animals don't. Unfortunately, the mandrill is out of luck. This is a type of large, hairy monkey with a colorful, but very bare, bottom. If you were a mandrill, being covered in hair might be toasty warm, but you'd have a very chilly backside.

Heaps of Hair

If you're lucky, you might wake up one day with hair like a musk ox, the hairiest of any animal. With two-foot-long (60-centimeter-long) hair all over your body, you could rock several amazing hairstyles all at once—pigtails, braids, curls, and a spiky Mohawk. The downside is that your hair would be really annoying to wash and brush every day, and imagine how blocked the drain in your bath would get from all that hair. Gross!

Fascinating Furry Facts
Take a look at these hair-raising facts:

- The American hairless terrier dog and Sphynx cat breeds have no fur at all.

- Sea otters have an amazing 15,500 hairs per square inch (100,000 hairs per square centimeter) of skin.

- Polar bears actually have colorless fur, but it reflects the light, which makes it appear white.

. . . YOUR SKIN COULD CHANGE COLOR?

Some people change the color of their hair to all kinds of wacky, bright shades, but you're pretty much stuck with the color of your skin. What if you weren't?

Hide-and-Seek

Some octopuses can change the color and pattern on their skin to match whatever's around them. If you had the power to change your skin, you could hide against brick walls or bookshelves and become a very successful top-secret spy. Why stop there? You could sneak into the movies for free by hiding in front of movie posters.

Sharp as a Shark

A shark's skin is covered with "dermal denticles."
These are hard spikes that are made of the same stuff
as teeth. If you had teeth all over your skin, you might
shave all the hair off your dog by just brushing past him.

Skin for Rainy Days

Lizards called frilled dragons
have a huge crest of colorful
skin around their necks, which
can stretch out to five times
wider than their heads. The
crests are shaped like upturned
umbrellas, which wouldn't be
very useful on a rainy day.

. . . YOU HAD TWO HEADS?

You know what they say—two heads are better than one. This isn't just a clever saying—it's almost true for some amazing animals.

Sleepy Head

A yellow-lipped sea krait snake has a tail that looks exactly like its head, which fools predators. If you had a trick head, you could take a snooze with your real head and keep the other looking bright and alert in class—no one would know the difference.

One Step Ahead

What if your parents appeared to have two pairs of eyes? Some birds have eye-like patterns on the backs of their heads, so it seems like they're watching you when they're not. Your devious deeds might come to an end if you had trouble telling whether you were being watched or not.

Tusk Tricks

Would you like a long tusk on your face like a male narwhal (a kind of whale)? You could pop marshmallows on the end to roast over the campfire. Toasty!

Head Check

Check out your head in the mirror and see how many of these fantastic features you have. If you can't check off any, chances are you're just a human.

☐ A rod with a dangling light on the end to attract prey, like a female anglerfish.

☐ Magnetic particles in your head to help you navigate, like a pigeon.

☐ No head at all! A chicken called Mike lived without a head for 18 months in Colorado.

☐ A bulgy forehead that conducts sound waves, allowing you to hear underwater, like a dolphin.

. . . YOU COULD CRUSH RIBS WITH A HUG?

Arms are useful things—you can reach for a snack or hug your little brother (when you feel like it), but what if your arms had superstrength or you had more than two of them?

Crushing Cuddles

The arms of a male chimpanzee are an amazing five times stronger than those of a human, and a big male mountain gorilla has a whopping eight-foot (two-and-a-half-meter) arm span. If your mom had the arm strength of a chimp and the mega arm span of a gorilla, not only could she sweep you and all your friends up in one big hug, but also she would probably give you all a good crushing if she were too enthusiastic.

HOW 1 HANDY

Flying Underwater

Swimming can be tough work. If you had flippers like a penguin, you could glide through the water like a bird flying through the air. Catching a tasty fish for your supper would be a breeze.

Arm-y Army

If two arms aren't enough to do all the things that you'd like to be able to do, how would you like to have eight arms, like an octopus? Better still, your arms would be covered in grippy suckers to cling on to things. You could play a video game, comb your hair, lift weights and brush your teeth all at the same time.

HOW
5
HANDY

. . . YOU GREW MORE LEGS AS YOU GOT OLDER?

You might think you get through life just fine with only two legs, but what if you had four, or six, or even *hundreds*? Or what if you had legs longer than anyone else you knew?

Loads of Legs

Millipedes and centipedes are well known for having many legs. But did you know that they grow more legs the older they get? If you sprouted a new pair of legs for every birthday, you'd get a lot of shoes for presents. And you'd really need them—especially if you were a rare type of Northern Californian millipede that has a whopping 750 legs.

HOW
4
HANDY

Lengthy Legs

Black-winged stilts are birds with legs one and a half times longer than the rest of their bodies. If you had such fantastically long legs, you'd be first pick for the basketball team—the only player who could make a slam dunk without jumping. Unfortunately, off the basketball court, you'd spend a great deal of time talking to the tops of people's heads.

. . . YOU COULD USE YOUR FEET TO HANG FROM THE CEILING?

Many people think that human feet are stinky and gross, but if our feet had some of these useful features, people might learn to love them.

Let's Hang Out

If you had feet like a sucker-footed bat, you could hang upside down from the ceiling without falling, thanks to suction pads on your feet. You could be generous and offer to help your dad paint the ceiling, or if you were feeling particularly mischievous, you could simply drop water balloons on your unsuspecting family.

A Stinky Pair

When dogs sweat, nearly all of it comes out of their feet. Feet are pretty stinky to begin with—how would you keep the stink at bay if you sweated in the same way?

ROTTEN
4
RATING

Famished Feet

Some feet aren't only used for walking. Horseshoe crabs use their spiny feet as teeth to "chew" their food. Imagine having to chew everything with your feet before putting it in your mouth. Your parents wouldn't be too happy if you had to get your feet out at the dinner table. They might also make you floss between your toes. Yuck!

. . . YOU HAD A FLY-SWATTING TAIL?

Many animals have tails. It's a little unfair that we humans don't, since they would be useful when you want to do something that arms and legs just can't handle.

Why Would You Want a Tail?

From swinging in the trees to swatting flies, there are a lot of reasons why a tail would come in handy.

- If you were a lizard, your tail would break off if a predator grabbed it, leaving you free to escape.

- Summertime picnics can be surrounded by buzzing flies. If you had a fly-swatting tail like a cow, one swift swish would show them who's boss.

- If you had a tail like most monkeys, you'd feel at home swinging carefree in the treetops. You'd also have somewhere to hide when your mom started bugging you to do your homework.

- If you were a squirrel, you wouldn't need a blanket to keep you warm while you slept—you could just wrap yourself in your cozy, bushy tail.

- Komodo dragons knock their prey down with their powerful tails. You might not have to catch your own food, but you could use a tail like this to take a swipe at someone helping himself to a tasty treat you had your eye on.

. . . *YOUR TAIL SHOWED YOUR FEELINGS?*

What's in a Wag?

Did you know that you can tell how a dog is feeling by the way it wags its tail? A wag to the left usually means that the dog is fearful or anxious. A wag to the right often signals that it is happy and excited. If you were a dog, you would probably wag your tail to the left when it's time to do homework and wag to the right when your dad sneaks some food to you under the kitchen table.

This Might Sting a Little

Even though its tail is called "the barb of death," a stingray is a gentle, usually passive fish—only using its tail to lash out at predators in self-defense. When a stingray feels threatened—by a shark, for instance—venom shoots through its tail and is efficiently delivered through the tail's sharply serrated and spiny edge. Sometimes part of the tail can break off during the scuffle, but the stingray won't be defenseless for long. The tail will grow back.

More Tail Tidbits

Can't get enough about tails? Here are some more facts for you:

- A crocodile stores fat from the food that it eats in its tail. If food gets scarce, it can go as long as 18 months without eating and survive on the fat.

- An antbear—or aardvark—uses its long, bushy tail as an umbrella when it gets caught in a rainstorm.

- A beaver uses its paddle-like tail to steer while swimming—not to build dams, as you might have thought.

. . . YOU WERE LEAFY LIKE A TREE?

Have you ever wished you had a crazy body part that made you stand out from the crowd? Would having a see-through head make you the envy of all your friends, or would they just call you an airhead?

Make like a Tree and Leave

A leafy sea dragon is a weird fish with what looks like leaves growing out of its body. When it's floating around in the ocean, it looks just like a piece of seaweed. This look could work perfectly well for you, too. If you had these leafy adornments, you could hang out in the park all day. No one would suspect that that odd-looking tree was playing hooky from school.

What an Airhead!

There is a deep-sea fish called the Pacific barreleye that has a see-through head. Pretty cool, wouldn't you say? Unless your friends started to have a conversation while looking right through you—very rude!

ROTTEN 4 RATING

Tentacle-Tastic

If you had the tickly 115-foot-long (35-meter-long) sticky tentacles of a lion's mane jellyfish, you could:

- Torture your sister by tickling her like crazy.

- Tie both your shoe-laces at the same time.

- Dip your tentacles in a jar of honey and lick them off—yum!

. . . but you'd have to be careful of your own sting!

. . . YOU HAD POP-OUT CLAWS?

Do you ever wish you had a built-in weapon that you could use to freak out your parents? What if you had claws on your hands or a saw for a nose? Getting out of chores would be a breeze.

A Wicked Weapon

Not only is a hairy frog quite hairy—which is odd enough for a frog—but it also has sharp claws that pop out of its "fingertips" when it's feeling particularly moody. With an instant weapon like this, you would be well on your way to becoming a superhero, and your mom would never make you clean your room again.

En Garde!

A male Hercules beetle has a big, pointy horn that he uses to fight other Hercules beetles. Arguments about who gets to use the bathroom first could get nasty.

Slice and Dice

Sawfish get their name because they have long, flat noses with little spikes along the edges. If you had this handy tool attached to your face, you wouldn't necessarily have to use it for fighting. You could be a great help to your parents, slicing and dicing the vegetables for dinner. Just watch out where you're pointing that thing . . .

HOW HANDY 3

. . . YOU HAD A KILLER KICK?

It would be cool to have a superhero's skills to fight crime and beat the bad guys. Which of these animal powers would you like to have?

The Killer Kicker

If you could kick like a horse, you could strike an attacker with the force of a bowling ball traveling at 80 miles (130 kilometers) an hour. One blow would send the thug flying so far that he'd never bother you again.

The Beaked Beater

If you had the daggerlike beak of a heron, you could spear bag-snatchers in one swift jab.

SCARY
4
SCORE

Python Man

A large python can disable its prey by squashing it in its coils. If you had this squeezing strength, you could capture villains with your coils.

More Marvellous Superpowers

The fun doesn't stop there. Check out some of these scary talents.

The Spurred Avenger:
Male platypuses have venom-filled spurs (sharp, horny growths) on their back legs.

Captain Venom:
One bite from an inland taipan snake contains enough venom to kill more than 100 people.

The Spiked Assassin:
Porcupines can run backward to skewer predators on their 14-inch (35-centimeter) quills.

Bullet Boy:
Being stung by a bullet ant is as painful as being shot with a real bullet.

. . . YOU HAD SUPER-SMELLY SELF-DEFENSE SKILLS?

Survival skills can be violent, clever, quick . . . or smelly. But no matter how repulsive they are, if your defense skills are successful, no attacker will want to come near you again.

Skunk Attack

Skunks scare off predators by squirting them with a horrible-smelling liquid from a gland on their backsides—disgusting but completely effective.

If you ever had to use this gross tactic, you could run away knowing that your attacker would smell disgusting for days to come.

Puke Patrol

If predators come too close to the nest of a type of seabird called a fulmar, it vomits fishy gunk over them. This would make a great neighborhood-watch tactic for humans. You could simply hide in a tree and vomit on thieves to deter them.

ROTTEN 4 RATING

Ka-Boom!

Asian termites stop predatory insects from entering their tunnels by blowing themselves up and blocking the way with their gooey insides. This is not recommended—you might save your house, but you'd also be a bit dead.

. . . YOU LOOKED LIKE A PINECONE?

Some animals have terrific hiding skills to protect them from predators. What if you could disguise yourself from being seen?

Camouflage Charge

Pangolins are African anteaters that are covered in large scales that make them look like pinecones. You might not like the idea of having rough, scaly skin, but you could easily hide nestled in a leafy forest. You'd also have wicked armor should you ever need to leap out and take your enemy by surprise. Pangolins can also emit a foul-smelling acid from their bottoms. Bonus!

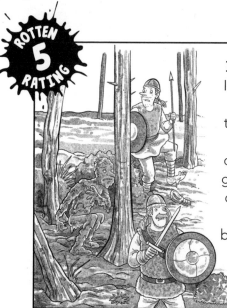

Disgusting Disguise
If you're really desperate for a disguise, do what the larva (wormlike baby insects) of a lily beetle does and give yourself a generous coating of your own poo. This would be very useful (although a bit smelly) when hiding in muddy forests.

What a Fluke!

The idea of camouflage is, of course, that you can hide from things that you don't want to find you. Strangely, fish that are infected with flukes (a type of parasite) sometimes go a bit bonkers and start showing off in front of a predator rather than hiding from it. If you had a nasty case of flukes, you might suddenly decide that doing cartwheels in front of a lion is a good idea.

. . . YOU LIVED IN A MOUND OF POO?

Luckily, you have warm clothes and a roof over your head—usually provided by your parents. But out in the wild, animals have to make their own living arrangements.

Do-It-Yourself

If you were a termite, it would be easy to build your own house. All you would need is some chewed-up wood, a little mud, and a generous helping of poo. Termite mounds can be a whopping 30 feet (nine meters) high. This is the equivalent of building a house nearly 10,000 (3,000 meters) high for a human. That's about as high as a mountain.

ROTTEN
5
RATING

Home Sweet Home

Tree houses can be fun to play in, but would you like living in a tree full time? Sociable weavers (sparrowlike birds) make huge communal nests that look like haystacks and can take up entire trees. Treetop living might sound ideal, but you're likely to get quite soggy when it rains.

Forest Fashions

Tailorbirds build their nests by sewing two leaves together, using plant fibers as threads and their beaks as needles. If you had these sewing skills, you could make all of your own clothes.

...YOU MADE STICKY SLIME?

Some animals have the ability to make amazing things. Of course, these skills are very useful to the animals, but for humans, how handy would they be?

Stuck Like Glue

Mussels make a gluelike substance to help them cling onto things, such as rocks and the bottoms of ships. Just one smear of this super-sticky stuff is enough to keep them stuck for over 50 years. Just imagine—if a person could produce this gluey stuff and accidentally stuck himself to the ceiling, he might be stuck there until he's old and wrinkly.

Caterpillar Costumes

Many people consider silk to be a very elegant fabric, but did you know that it comes from glands inside a caterpillar's mouth? It might be a little embarrassing if you suddenly started spewing out strands of silk from your mouth, but just consider the possibilities. You could . . .

- offer your services to a dressmaker—you might even get some fashionable freebies.

- spin webs like a spider to catch any pesky flies in your house.

- swing from the rooftops like a superhero, using homemade ropes of silk.

. . . YOU COULD LIFT A TRUCK?

There are lots of animals that can lift far more than their own body weight. The Hercules beetle, for example, can lift an amazing 850 times its own weight.

Heavyweights

If you could lift as much as the Hercules beetle relative to your body weight, it would be like lifting 143,000 pounds (65,000 kilograms)—that's not just one truck, but several. The most a man has ever lifted is a measly 580 pounds (263 kilograms). Here are some other amazingly heavy things you could lift:

- 20 baby blue whales
- 30,000 bricks
- 8 Tyrannosaurus rexes
- over 250,000 rolls of toilet paper
- 2 fighter jets
- 5 double-decker buses
- more than a million chocolate bars
- 2,500 poodles

Flying Fit

Do you have a lot of heavy books to carry to school? This would be no problem if you were an eagle. You could just fly, skipping the traffic jams, and your feet would have the strength to carry a bag that weighs half your own weight.

Champion Chewers

A spotted hyena's jaws are strong enough to chew up a saucepan. If you had these mega-strong jaws and were still peckish after your dinner, you could just munch on the saucepan it was cooked in—one less thing to clean up. Hyenas don't eat saucepans, of course. Instead, they use their jaws to crush animal bones.

. . . YOU WERE AS FAST AS A CHEETAH?

How would you like to run across the country in a couple of days or outswim a motorboat? The super speed of some animals is enough to leave you breathless.

Rapid Runners

A cheetah can dash at a spectacular 62 miles (100 kilometers) an hour. If you could maintain such an awesome speed, you could run across the United States in under two days. You couldn't slow down or take a break, of course, so you'd need to take a whole lot of water with you.

Perfect Pecker

Woodpeckers can strike a tree at a rate of 22 pecks a second. If you were lucky enough to have a beak and be as fast, your skills would make you the envy of everyone in woodworking class.

HOW **3** HANDY

Swift Swimmers

The fastest fish around is a sailfish, which can zoom through the water at a speedy 68 miles (110 kilometers) an hour. As its name suggests, this super-quick fish has a large fin on its back that sticks up like a sail. If you had the swimming skills of a sailfish, you could easily outswim a motorboat.

. . . YOU COULD "FLY" LIKE AN OSTRICH?

More Speedy Critters

We're not slowing down just yet. Here are some more ultrafast animals that will definitely leave you in the dust.

- Standing seven to nine feet tall, ostriches may not be able to fly, but they have two toes on each foot that make them agile and speedy birds on the ground. These African birds—the largest in the world—can reach speeds of around 45 miles (72 kilometers) an hour.

- Ruby-throated hummingbirds beat their wings 53 times per second—so fast that they make the humming sound after which they are named. Hummingbirds can fly 35 miles (56 kilometers) an hour and can reach speeds of up to 50 miles (80 kilometers) an hour when diving. And get this: they can even fly upside down and backward.

- Tiger beetles are aggressive predators who run so fast that their eyes can't keep up and they lose their sight. Now that's fast! They run in short, quick bursts, stopping just long enough to let their eyes catch up and determine the position of their prey before taking off again.

Not So Fast

The sloth is the slowest mammal on the planet. Sloths spend most of their time hanging from tree branches because they can only travel about five feet (one and a half meters) per minute. In that same minute:

- a cockroach can crawl 176 feet (54 meters).

- a human can walk 264 feet (80 meters).

- a greyhound can run 3,960 feet (1,200 meters).

- a quarter horse can gallop 4,400 feet (1,340 meters).

. . . YOU COULD JUMP OVER A SKYSCRAPER?

You may have tried the high jump in gym class or maybe even seen Olympic athletes do it, but that is nothing compared to the heights that some animals can reach.

Jumping Journeys

There is a small insect called a froghopper that can jump 28 inches (70 centimeters) straight up in the air. That might not sound terribly high, but the equivalent for a person would mean leaping over a skyscraper. Getting to work every morning would be easy—and a lot more fun than driving a car.

HOW HANDY 4

Aim High

A serval (an African wildcat) can jump 10 feet (three meters) in the air to grab passing birds. This is the equivalent of a human jumping almost 16 feet (five meters). If you had the super-jumping skills of a serval, you'd be sure to win a gold medal. You wouldn't have to grab a bird on your way up—unless you really wanted to.

Leap of Faith

The day after baby wood ducks hatch, they have to jump out of the tree where their nest is before they can fly. If they are lucky, they have a soft landing and don't hurt themselves.

. . . YOU COULD CLIMB UP WINDOWS?

Unless you're a daredevil rock climber, you probably spend most of your time walking around on the ground. However, for some climbing critters, the ground is old news.

Fly Feet

Flies have tiny hairs on their feet that make them ultra-grippy. They can even walk on windows by gripping the glass. In case you ever find yourself with such a super ability, here are some dos and don'ts:

DO

- Make sure your neighbors are out before you climb up their windows.

- Wear a helmet if you plan to climb very high.

- Be wary of low-flying planes.

DON'T

- Wear shoes, or the hairs on your feet won't work.

- Jump! Gravity doesn't work that way—you'll only go down.

- Be surprised if your parents ground you—literally!

Great Geckos

If you could walk up and down walls like a gecko (a type of small lizard), the need for ladders would be a thing of the past. You could make a lot of money with your own painting and decorating company, as wallpapering a room would be a breeze.

Scale with Scales

Many snakes are skilled climbers, gripping surfaces with the raised scales on their bellies. If you had these climbing scales, you could go rock climbing without safety ropes—what a daredevil!

. . . YOU COULD CLIMB WITH YOUR MOUTH?

Now That's Fishy

There's a kind of catfish in Venezuela that can do more than just swim. Check out its underside, and you'll see its mouth and a pair of super-flexible, leglike fins. This crafty catfish uses its extra "legs" and giant, sucking mouth to attach itself to and climb slippery rocks in the region's fast-flowing rivers—even catfish need to take a break every now and then.

Climb on Up

Here are some more curiosities about climbing creatures:

- Koala bears are so friendly that they have been known to climb a tourist's leg for a quick cuddle.

- The curve of a cat's claws helps it climb up trees with ease, but getting back down is another story. Unable go down head-first, they usually have to back down or jump—or wait to be rescued.

- Mountain goats are lucky to have pliable hooves with soft, rubbery pads that help them climb the craggy rocks of a steep mountainside.

- Coconut crabs are the largest terrestrial—meaning they live on land—crabs on the planet. They can grow to be up to three feet (one meter) wide and weigh around nine pounds (four kilograms). When these giants aren't burrowing in their cozy homes underground, they're climbing trees up to 20 feet (six meters) high to crack open one of their favorite snacks—you guessed it, coconuts!

. . . YOU COULD SURVIVE SUBZERO TEMPERATURES?

When it's cold outside, you probably have to bundle up to keep warm. But what if you could survive whatever the weather?

Frozen Solid
Woolly bear caterpillars in the Arctic spend ten months of the year frozen solid. If you did this, you'd only have to go to school two months out of the year.

Out of This World

Tardigrades are microscopic creatures that can cope with temperatures from as low as -459°F (−273°C) and as high as 304°F (151°C). They can even survive in outer space. If you were this robust, you could take a holiday that would be literally out of this world. All you'd need to do is hitch a ride on a rocket ship.

A Hare-y Situation

An arctic hare may look like a regular ol' rabbit, but it is specially equipped to live in the harsh Northern Tundra winters. It doesn't hibernate during the cold months, and its thick fur changes colors with the seasons. In the winter, its coat is pure white, offering good camouflage in the snow. In the spring, its coat turns a blue-ish gray, which helps it blend in with the rocky terrain.

Sweet Dreams

When it gets sleepy, a white fox wraps its big, bushy tail around its body like a blanket, which protects it from the freezing Arctic temperatures. If you were a white fox, you'd never have to lug your sleeping bag to another slumber party again.

. . . YOU LIVED BETWEEN YOUR DAD'S LEGS?

Thanks, Dad!

How would you feel about standing outside in -40°F (−40°C) for 64 days? You probably wouldn't jump at the chance, but male emperor penguins do this every year, while looking after an egg between their legs when their mates go in search of food. Would you like being crammed between your dad's knees for over two months in the freezing cold?

So, You Want to Live like a Penguin?
Here are some of the other crazy things
you'd have to do if you lived like a penguin in
freezing Antarctica.

- Huddle together for warmth with your massive group of penguin friends—up to several hundred.

- Be careful not to fall out of your dad's brood patch—a featherless patch of warm skin—you'd freeze to death in a matter of minutes.

- Dive for food to depths of over 550 meters in the freezing Antarctic waters.

- Eat food regurgitated, or puked up, by your mom and dad. Yum!

- Walk mostly on your heels—using your tail to keep balanced—in order to make as little contact as possible with the freezing-cold ground.

. . . YOU COULD FLY AS HIGH AS A PLANE?

If beating a world record is on the top of your to-do list, take a look at some of these strange animal records. They might just give you some inspiration.

Highest Flier

The ability to fly is probably at the top of a lot of people's wish lists, but it doesn't come without its perils. The highest-flying bird on record is a vulture. It hit a plane that was flying at 37,000 feet (11,277) meters high. Ouch!

Longest-Living

It's possible that bowhead whales can live forover 200 years, making them the longest-living mammals on the planet. If you could reach this age, your birthday cake would have to be massive to hold all of the candles. Would you have enough puff left to blow them all out?

Longest Tongue

A chameleon's tongue can be up to twice the length of its body. It can whip out of and then back into its mouth in a speedy 0.7 seconds to snatch up prey. You could easily sneak that last slice of cake without anyone noticing.

HOW
3
HANDY

. . . YOU COULDN'T SPEAK?

If you didn't communicate by talking, you might wonder how on earth you'd get your point across. It turns out that animals have some of the strangest ways of "speaking" that you can imagine.

Could You Repeat That?

If you didn't have a voice, you might want to try communicating like a grasshopper. Grasshoppers rub their legs against their abdomens to make the chirps that they use to "speak" to each other. The only problem is, no one would understand what you were saying—apart from grasshoppers, that is!

HOW HANDY 1

Take a Bow

What if you saw little kids politely bowing to each other in the playground? This is what dogs do when they want to play—they bow deeply to each other. How polite!

On the Trail

Termites leave a scent trail to tell each other where to find food. If you could do this, you'd certainly be very popular with all your friends, but you'd have to make sure you had your fill before the your friends got there.

. . . LIFE WERE A MUSICAL?

If humans communicated like animals, everyday life would become very exciting and strange. You'd certainly never be bored.

A Whale of a Time

Whales communicate with song, even though their clicks, squeals, and long, drawn-out groans may not sound very musical to us. If all of your teachers taught their lessons in song, school would be a lot more lively, don't you think? And by whale-singing standards, it wouldn't even matter if they couldn't sing very well.

Light Entertainment

A firefly squid can light up parts of its body to impress other firefly squids—and scare off predators. If you and your friends could do this, you could communicate secretly in the dark with Morse code, and you could tell your little brother to stay out of your room.

Colorful Language

Lots of animals use color to communicate. Some—like peacocks—flaunt their bright colors in order to attract a mate. Others have colors that serve as warnings to their predators. The red stripes on a venomous coral snake signal to hungry birds that it would not make a good snack and should be left alone.

. . . YOU SPOKE WITH YOUR EYES?

Say What?

Animals communicate in so many different ways. There are probably just as many different types of "talking" as there are animals on the planet.

- Nightjars are birds that fly at night. They signal in the dark by flashing their white wing feathers at each other. You can confuse a nightjar by waving a white hankie in the air.

- Birds migrating at night tweet constantly so that no one gets separated from the group.

- Howler monkeys communicate with bloodcurdling screeches. Imagine how your teachers would feel if that was how you and your friends chatted with each other.

- Elephants have a secret language that they use to communicate to each other over very long distances. These sounds can travel for miles and are so low-pitched that humans can't even hear them.

- Prairie dogs (a type of rodent) squeak to warn each other of danger. The pitches of the squeaks let others know exactly how scary the situation is.

- Gazelles lift their tails and flash the white fur of their behinds to warn others when a predator—like a cheetah—is nearby.

. . . YOU FELL IN LOVE WITH FARTS?

Most people consider farting rude, smelly, and something that should be avoided in public at all costs, but some animals are unashamed of their tremendous gases.

Fabulous Farts

Farts—they are wonderful things if you're a southern pine beetle. The smell of the female beetle's farts is highly attractive to a male. So, ladies, forget the perfume or bubble bath, all you need is what nature gave you—a healthy dose of digestive gas.

ROTTEN 3 RATING

Speak Fart

Some fish may use farts to communicate with each other. Would you swap learning French or Spanish for a lesson in the fine art of farting if humans did the same thing?

SMART 3 POINTS

Wipe Out

Dogs' digestive systems can't digest fart-tastic beans very well. If you had the gut of a dog and ate a plate of beans, you would fart huge volumes of gas—enough to seriously gross out an elevator full of people.

. . . YOU WALKED UPSIDE DOWN?

It's no fun being ill, but there are some horrible diseases that affect animals in strange and intriguing ways.

Handy Standing

A swim bladder is a gas-filled organ in a fish that helps it stay afloat in water. A fish with a diseased swim bladder will often swim upside down. If people had this condition, they might walk upside down, on their hands. On the bright side, if you ever felt like joining the circus, you'd have no problem finding a job.

Hold Still . . .

Some animal diseases might sound cool and fairly harmless, but there are others that you'll want to avoid like the plague. Sadly, when bee larvae pick up a fungal disease called stonebrood, the soft and squishy larvae to turn hard like stones, almost like they've been mummified. If you were in danger of turning to stone, not only would it be terrifying, but it could also be really embarrassing. What if you were stuck while picking your nose, sniffing your armpits, or something equally cringe-worthy?

. . . YOU HAD A PARASITE FOR A TONGUE?

When you're being annoying, your big brother or sister might call you a "parasite," a creature that will use another living thing for food and protection all its life.

Lick with a Woodlouse

The spotted rose snapper fish can suffer from a woodlouse-like parasite that destroys its tongue. Eventually the fish uses the parasite as a replacement tongue. If this happened to you, it would be pretty disgusting—plus you wouldn't even be able to taste your food.

Tropical Vampires

Mockingbirds in the Galápagos Islands peck holes in the skin of sea lions to drink their blood. Forget about going to the beach to have a relaxing afternoon!

Nutrient Nabbers

Believe it or not, some pesky parasites steal nutrients from other animals. Male angler fish attach themselves to the much larger female angler fish and absorb nutrients from them. If human males were parasites like this, imagine how annoying it would be if you were just running to the store and were bombarded by a horde of tiny men trying to nab your nutrients.

. . . YOU COULD EAT ROCKS FOR BREAKFAST?

Do you think you have a strong stomach? Maybe you can gobble down a fiery hot jalepeño pepper without breaking a sweat, but are your guts tough enough to handle a diet of rocks?

Rock 'n' Rolls

Ostriches have the perfect solution for indigestion. They simply swallow a bunch of grit and rocks, which sit in their stomach and help grind up the tough plants that they eat. This might come in handy when you want to pig out at a barbecue, but you'd probably break a few of your teeth trying to munch on rocks afterward.

... YOUR GUTS WERE ON DISPLAY?

Usually guts are neatly tucked away inside the human body, but what if they were on display for the world to see? Yuck!

Weird Windpipes

Ever bitten off more than you can chew—literally? If you were like some snakes, you'd be able to pop your windpipe out of your mouth to make room to swallow massive things, like a whole deer. But maybe you'd prefer to stick with a tasty burger.

X-tra Special

The X-ray tetra fish has a see-through body, so you can see all of its inner workings. If you were transparent, everyone would be able to see what you'd just eaten for lunch.

ROTTEN 4 RATING

. . . YOU ATE 850 SAUSAGES AT ONE TIME?

If you love stuffing yourself silly, you might like to have a huge stomach like a blue whale. You'd never feel full.

Meaty Menu

A lion can scarf 75 pounds (34 kilograms) of meat at one time. Here's what might be on the menu if you could undertake such a meaty meal:

- 850 sausages or barbecue ribs.
- 220 steaks or pork chops.
- 24 roast chickens.
- 1,500 meatballs.

Aren't You Full Yet?

Do your parents ever tell you to stop snacking? They should be pleased that they don't have a giant panda for a child who. A giant panda will spend 15 hours a day just munching bamboo.

Get Your Fill of Krill

Blue whales feed almost entirely on tiny shrimp-like sea animals called krill, and can get through 40 million of them every day. If you had to eat only one thing—and this much of it—the very idea of eating might bore your brains out.

. . . YOU COULD TACKLE A LIONESS?

Hopefully you've never eaten anything bigger than could fit on your dinner plate. But what if you could devour something twice your size and still feel hungry the next day?

A Lion for Lunch

Stoats—which are like weasels—regularly catch and eat rabbits more than twice as big as they are. Rabbits may not be particularly ferocious, but sizewise this is about the same as a fully-grown man munching on a lioness. Would you be brave enough to give it a try, or would you rather leave it to your dad?

Super Swallower

If you were a black swallower fish, you could swallow something up to ten times your weight—whole! Your stomach would be able to expand to fit it in, but you might not be able to fit into your jeans.

Outside In

A hagfish chews its way into a larger fish, then eats it from the inside. If you were a hagfish, instead of getting a tasty steak on your plate, you'd have to eat your way into a cow to get it.

ROTTEN
5
RATING

. . . YOU ATE A PLATE OF JELLYFISH?

From poisonous jellyfish to steering wheels, animals have been known to munch on mysterious things. Do any of these snacks sound yummy to you?

Jelly Belly

Sea turtles happily eat jellyfish—stinging tentacles and all. Usually this sort of crazy behavior would be deadly for a human, but if you had a sea turtle's strong stomach, you could add a dash of sauce and a generous helping of meatballs to your jellyfish dish. It might look no different than a big plate of spaghetti.

ROTTEN
4
RATING

Tasty Trees

Elephants eat the wood and bark of trees, as well as the leaves. If such a treat tickled your fancy and your stomach could digest it, you could forget taking a picnic basket to the park and just munch on the nearby trees instead!

Bins with Fins

Tiger sharks are known as "bins with fins" because they will eat everything and anything they encounter, even swallowing inedible objects. Anyone want to chow down on a steering wheel?

. . . YOUR MOM PUKED IN YOUR MOUTH?

Animals can do some pretty disgusting things, but *eating* gross things might be one step too far. You'd have to be starving to indulge in some of these sickening snacks.

Vile Vomit

Some mother birds feed their babies by eating the food first and then vomiting it back up into their little ones' mouths. It's called regurgitation. Human babies need feeding more frequently than adults, so if your mom fed you like this, that would be a whole lot of puking. If she fed you what birds eat, here are some of the things you might have to force down:

- seeds and berries.
- raw fish.
- a ball of insects.
- worms.

ROTTEN 5 RATING

Fine Dining . . . Down the Toilet

Magpie birds regularly pick through piles of animal poo, looking for undigested food. If you did the same, you'd have to eat all of your meals in the bathroom and would probably become seriously ill from all of the nasty bacteria.

Brains, Anyone?

In a remote cave in Hungary, scientists discovered that a group of small birds called great tits got so hungry that they visited a bat roost and pecked the sleeping bats' brains out. What if, feeling like a midnight snack, you popped over to your friend's house to nibble on his brain? You probably wouldn't be invited over again!

. . . SOMEONE DRANK YOUR SWEAT?

There's nothing better than a cool drink on a hot day—unless of course that drink happens to be human sweat . . .

Stinking Drinking

Sweat bees live in hot countries and land on people's faces to drink their sweat. What if every time you got a bit hot and sweaty you had to fend off other people swooping in for a tasty lick? Gym class at school would be a nightmare.

ROTTEN
4
RATING

... SOMEONE ATE YOUR SKIN?

Most humans don't think twice about eating animals. Many animals, such as dust mites, feel exactly the same about nibbling on unsuspecting humans.

ROTTEN
5
RATING

A Flaky Feast

Imagine snuggling into bed one night and suddenly discovering your little brother beneath your covers, nibbling on your dead flakes of skin. This is what dust mites do. It would be hard to sleep after this disgusting discovery.

Cootchie Cootchie—Ouch!

Imagine if human babies had the bone-crushing bite of a snapping turtle. These creatures have very strong jaws and wouldn't think twice about snapping your finger clean off.

. . . YOU DRANK OVER 25 GALLONS OF WATER?

You might not think there's much to drinking other than gulping down a glass of your favorite juice or fizzy drink. However, for some animals, the art of drinking can be much more creative than that.

Thirsty Work

Drinking is thirsty work, especially if you're a camel that can gulp down over 25 gallons (100 liters) of water at one time and then not have to drink again for over a week. If you had this ability, you would make a great desert-rescue hero for stranded travelers.

Make a Splash

Drinking like an elephant would be great fun. They suck water into their trunks, then squirt it into their mouths. Water fight!

Fantastic Drinking Facts

Do you think all animals drink water?
Think again . . .

- Seabirds drink seawater but get rid of the excess salt through their nostrils.

- Some butterflies drink juices from animal droppings.

- When there's nothing to drink, some lizards reabsorb water from the urine in their bladders.

- Malaysian tree shrews drink alcoholic nectar—the equivalent of nine glasses of strong beer a day.

. . . YOU HAD TO DRINK BLOOD TO SURVIVE?

Fear not—the blood drinkers of the world mean no harm with their sipping habits. Blood is simply full of the nutrients that they need to survive—just like we couldn't live without water. Most of the time, these critters fill up and go on their way. Sometimes they leave behind some itchy spots, which is probably just their way of saying thank you.

Sneaky Little Sippers

Almost all of the blood drinkers out there are insects, but there is one mammal in the mix.

- Leeches are blood-drinking worms that have suckers on both ends. They are speedy slurpers and can drink five times their body weight in only 20 minutes. They don't eat often, though, and can go up to a year and a half between meals

- Fleas have spring-loaded legs that allow them to jump 200 times their body length. That's the same as you being able to jump the length of more than two football fields! A flea at a dog park could just jump from dog to dog without even having to touch the ground.

- Male vampire moths in Siberia pass up yummy fruit juices for blood. They use their hook-and-barb-lined tongues to pierce a mammal's skin and drink until full (burp).

- Candirus are tiny cannibals who live in the Amazon River. These transparent fish—a type of catfish—snuggle into the blood-rich gills of other fish and nibble and slurp up.

- Vampire bats are the only mammals that live on blood. Instead of sucking the blood from cows, pigs, horses, and birds, vampire bats make a little cut with their razor-sharp teeth and then lick up the pooling blood with their tongues.

. . . YOU WRESTLED WITH YOUR FOOD?

Some people like to eat meat that is nearly raw. But how about so raw it can still moo? If people ate their food while it was still alive like some animals do, the world would be a wilder place.

Rip 'n' Roll

Crocodiles rip bits off creatures while they're still alive by violently shaking and rolling about. This is called a death roll. It's rather like wrestling—with a violent twist. If you had to go through this ordeal with a cow every time you wanted a beef burger, you just might become a vegetarian.

HOW
1
HANDY

Talking Food

Grass snakes swallow frogs whole, and these frogs can sometimes be heard squealing for several minutes after they've been eaten. If this happened to you, it would be far more embarrassing than your stomach growling loudly.

IT'S DARK IN HERE!

Chase Down Your Chow

Orcas (also known as killer whales) take bites out of their prey while chasing it. If you really feel you must chase down your dinner in this way, remember to take these essentials along with you:

- When chasing sheep, take dental floss to remove the wool from your teeth.

- If you're going pig chasing, wear rain boots—you're likely to be running through some muddy areas.

- If you're chasing birds, good luck—unless you have wings!

. . . YOU HAD TO DANCE FOR YOUR DINNER?

If you had to catch your own food, you might have to do any number of crazy things to lure it to you—some more strange than others . . .

Shall We Dance?

What if dancing weren't just a fun thing to do, but were actually essential for your survival? Weasels are said to perform a hypnotizing "dance" to confuse their prey before they pounce. Imagine if your parents made you dance for your dinner every day. Cringe!

The Webbed Assassin

One kind of assassin bug will ping the webs of spiders until they come to investigate—then eat them. This would be a very tiring thing to have to do every day. Not only would you have to wait around for your food, but you'd also have to learn to play a web like a harp.

Aim and Spit

Archer fish knock flies into the water by spitting at them. Your parents probably tell you not to spit in public, but they couldn't get mad if it were the only way you could catch a good meal.

. . . YOU COULD EJECT YOUR STOMACH?

You might not enjoy cooking, but perhaps you should be thankful that preparing your next meal doesn't involve any of the following disgusting practices.

Hard to Stomach

When a starfish finds a shellfish that it wants to eat, it ejects its stomach directly on top of its victim. If you had this spectacular talent, it probably wouldn't be a great idea to do it at a fancy dinner party—it's a bit worse than slurping your soup.

ROTTEN
4
RATING

Look Out!

A cunning way to catch your dinner would be to copy a bearded vulture. It drops rocks on tortoises from a great height. Imagine your poor victims: One minute they'd be minding their own business and the next thing—SPLAT—boulders would fall on their heads.

Slime, Glorious Slime

Velvet worms squirt slime at their prey. This would be one way to make sure you got the last helping of food—no one would want to eat slime- covered snacks.

. . . YOUR MOM ATE YOUR DAD'S HEAD?

Everyone argues sometimes—moms and dads, brothers and sisters—but in the wild world of animals, some males really have to watch their step, or things can get deadly.

Don't Lose Your Head

Isn't it gross when your mom and dad kiss or hold hands? Consider yourself lucky that your mom doesn't have the habits of an insect called a praying mantis. After getting romantic, the female sometimes bites off her partner's head. Just be grateful that your dad still has his head—some poor praying mantis kids can't say the same about theirs.

All Tied Up

A male lynx spider will tie up a female with his silk to stop her from eating him. What if your dad had to do that whenever he took your mom out?

Dance for Your Life!

Male wolf spiders do special dances that (sometimes) stop the females from eating them. What if your dad had to dance for your mom to make sure he lived to see another day? It might be entertaining for you, but your poor dad wouldn't find it much fun.

. . . YOU ATE YOUR MOM'S SKIN?

Hopefully you consider your mom more than just a source of delicious meals. Motherhood wouldn't be much fun if kids liked to munch on their moms' at every available chance.

Skinny Supper

Your mom might let you get away with all sorts of naughty things, but what would she say if you decided to take a nibble of her skin? A baby caecilian—which looks like a worm but is actually related to a frog—survives its first few days of life by eating its mother's skin. She even grows an extra-thick layer of skin for this purpose. Your own mom probably wouldn't thank you for gnawing on her arm while she's trying to read the newspaper.

Newborn Gnawers

In some spider species, the first thing babies do after hatching is eat their mother. That's a nice way to thank you poor old mom!

Monster Babies

Probably the most unlucky mother in the animal world is the gall midge (a type of flying insect). Her gruesome babies are so impatient to be born that they eat their way out of her body. Just imagine . . .

SCARY 5 SCORE

. . . YOUR MOM HAD A MILLION BABIES?

Your mom might tell you how special you are by saying that you're one in a million, but what if you actually had a million brothers and sisters?

So Many Siblings

There's no doubt about it that brothers and sisters can be extremely annoying. If you're lucky, you might only have one or two, but if you were a mackerel, your mom could give birth to between 300,000 and 1,500,000 babies—all at the same time. That's a lot of diaper changing and mopping up of spit-up for your poor parents.

Back babies

Pregnant Surinam toads carry babies under the skin on their backs. If human women had to carry their babies like this, they'd be forced to walk hunched over as their back bulges got bigger and bigger. On the plus side, once fully grown, the babies can just pop out from the skin on a toad's back. Sounds easy, right?

More Bizarre Births

- Quails grow up fast. These birds can have babies when they are just six weeks old.

- Greenflies don't need to mate to have babies and are often already pregnant when they are born.

- The common tenrec (a small furry creature from Madagascar) can produce—and successfully look after—30 babies in one litter.

. . . YOU WERE BROUGHT UP BY A LION?

When adults want to adopt a baby, they usually want a human baby. Some animals, though, don't seem to care what species they get.

Ferocious Foster Family

In Kenya, one unusual lioness repeatedly "adopted" and looked after baby antelopes, which would normally be lunch for a lion. If you were brought up by lions, you'd have a very different life:

- You'd sleep in a thicket or den.

- You would be carried by the scruff of your neck.

- You'd be at risk of leopard or hyena attacks.

- You might have up to four very ferocious brothers and sisters to play with.

Baby Snatchers

If a female emperor penguin loses her baby, she might attempt to adopt her neighbor's. Luckily humans don't do this, or your mom might try to adopt the kid next door if you were ever late coming home from school.

Babysitting Bees

Cuckoo bees lay their eggs in the nests of other bees. Watch out—if you don't behave yourself, your mom might be tempted to dump you and your brothers and sisters off at a stranger's house.

. . . YOU WERE A KID FOREVER?

Wouldn't it be great if you never had to grow up, just like Peter Pan? But think carefully—it could be frustrating if no one ever took you seriously.

Kidding Around

Domestic cats can act like kittens for all of their lives. This may be because in the wild their parents would have encouraged them to live on their own. If you could act like a kid your entire life, you could play in the park all day long, eat ice cream for breakfast, and never have to worry about getting a job.

HOW HANDY 5

Forever Young

When it's a baby, a salamander (a type of amphibian) has gills, which are organs that allow some creatures to breathe underwater. Most salamanders lose their gills when they become adults, but a type of salamander called an axolotl has gills like a baby all of its life. Imagine looking like a baby all of your life and having to convince everyone that you were really an adult.

Growing Pains

The fulmar (a kind of seabird) looks just the same at one year old as it does when it's 50. How tiresome would it be to never look like you are growing even one day older?

. . . YOUR BED WERE MADE OF UNDERWEAR?

What would your ideal bed be made of? Soft feathers? A fluffy cloud? Count yourself lucky that you don't have to sleep in rotting garbage or on top of old underwear.

Where's the Underwear?

Red kites are birds of prey that like to decorate their nests with things they collect. Some have been known to steal people's underwear to make their nests extra colorful. If you collected underwear to decorate your bedroom, your mom probably wouldn't be thrilled if she opened your door to find a heap of underpants where your bed used to be. She probably already gets fed up with having to pick up your clothes, let alone other people's that you've decided to collect.

Spit 'n' Sleep

The edible-nest swiftlet is a small bird that makes a nest from its own spit. The spit dries out to make a solid crust. Would you like sleeping in a bed made of your mom and dad's spit?

Cot of Rot

What if you were born in a pile of rotting garbage? The malleefowl (a chickenlike bird) buries its eggs in a big pile of decaying vegetation. The rotting process provides warmth, which helps the eggs hatch. If you were born in a trash can, it might be cozy, but it would definitely be a bit stinky.

ROTTEN
3
RATING

. . . YOUR DAD TRIED TO EAT YOU?

What's your mom or dad's favorite food? A juicy steak or a tasty pizza? What if their favorite food wasn't food at all—but YOU?

Ferocious Fathers

If you get on your dad's nerves, the worst he might do is tell you to go to your room. Thank your lucky stars that you're not a bass fish. A male will sometimes guard his babies carefully for a few days, then suddenly start eating them.

SCARY SCORE 5

Babies For Breakfast

Goldfish eat their own eggs. If you were in danger of being eaten from the moment you popped into the world, you'd really have to rely on a nurse at the hospital to save you from your hungry mom.

Signs Your Mom Is a Panda

If you know any twins, they probably complain when their parents dress them in the same clothes. But if they were brought up by a giant panda, their mom would pick her favorite and let the other one starve. If you're a twin, make sure you watch out for the following:

- Your mom starts to regularly weigh and measure you and your twin. A panda will size up her twins and select the strongest to live.

- When you wake up, your twin has already been washed, brushed, and fed by your mom, and there is only a stale piece of bread left over for you.

- Your house is full of pictures of a cute baby—but it's not you.

- Your mom seems to forget your birthday, even though it's on the same day as your twin's.

- Your twin starts to get more friends than you, because you're becoming a bit dirty and smelly.

. . . YOUR PARENTS ABANDONED YOU?

If you have wonderful people who take care of you and tell you how special you are, you should feel very lucky. Some creatures in the animal kingdom are lucky just to have anyone look after them at all.

Are You There, Mom?

If you hatched out of an egg on a deserted beach and your mom was nowhere to be seen, do you think you could find your way home? Turtles bury their eggs in the sand and then leave them there to hatch. By the time the babies hatch and crawl out of the sand, the moms are long gone. If you ever found yourself in this predicament, let's just hope that you would have lots of brothers and sisters to help you out.

See Ya!

Swallows migrate to Africa for the winter. If they still have babies in their nests when migration time comes, they will simply leave them. What if your parents went on holiday without you? You'd have the whole house to yourself, could eat as many snacks as you wanted and watch whatever you like on TV. Brilliant!

Thanks, Mom

Most birds look after their babies for at least a couple of weeks, but megapode chicks have to fend for themselves from day one. Imagine if you'd had to wash your own clothes and cook your own meals as a baby.

HOW HANDY

. . . YOUR PARENTS COATED YOU IN VENOM?

It's no secret: parents can be extremely embarrassing. If they aren't kissing you in public, then they're calling you baby names in front of your friends. Could it get any worse? Yes . . .

Lethal Lick

A slow loris (a small mammal) has a gland on its arm that oozes venom. It licks up this venom and coats its babies with it to keep them from being eaten by predators. If your mom did this to you, it might keep you from being munched on, but it certainly wouldn't help you make any friends.

ROTTEN
3
RATING

Follow the Leader

Shrew families travel around in "caravans," where each baby holds onto the back of the one in front, using its teeth. How would you like it if your little brothers and sisters had to hold onto your T-shirt wherever you went?

Dinner's Ready!

Cheetahs bring live baby antelopes to their cubs for them to learn how to chase and kill. If at mealtimes your mom put a live sheep on the table, you'd either have to learn some cheetah tactics or go hungry.

. . . YOU WERE PAMPERED BY EVERYONE?

Having overprotective parents can be irritating, but they only do it because they love you. Try to relax and enjoy the attention—and be thankful that they don't take things as far as some animals do.

Perfectly Pampered

How would you like to arrive home from school to find your mom, dad, brothers, and sisters waiting to attend to your every whim? This is the celebrity treatment that a baby moorhen (a type of waterbird) receives. It is lovingly fed and cared for not only by its mom and dad, but also by its older brothers and sisters.

HOW HANDY 5

The Booby Prize

Male dyak fruit bats are the only male mammals that have milk-producing breasts, so both moms and dads feed their young. Just imagine your own dad with a pair of breasts . . .

Never Fly the Nest

A baby albatross sits in its nest for nearly a year, being brought food by both parents. This may not seem like a very long time, but baby birds usually leave their nests much earlier. Just try to imagine a grown adult still being cared for like a baby.

. . . YOUR NEIGHBORHOOD SHARED ONE TOILET?

Humans seem to enjoy living together—it's nice to have a bit of company. But what if you had to share one toilet with loads of people, or you didn't even have your own bed? Nightmare!

Get in Line

Living with a big family might mean that you argue over who gets to use the bathroom first in the morning. If this is one of your pet peeves, thank your lucky stars that you're not a raccoon. These furry critters share a toilet with all of their neighbors. If you had to do the same, not only would you have to wait ages to use it, but also the smell would be unbearable.

ROTTEN **4** RATING

Sleepy Squeezes

On cold winter nights, birds called wrens will squeeze into the same roosting hole for warmth. Up to 34 of them have been seen going into one nest box together. Would you enjoy sharing a bed with 34 people?

One Too Many

Guillemots are birds that nest in huge colonies, packing tightly onto cliff ledges. If there's room to sit down, there's room to have a family. What if all the houses on your street had swarms of kids on every windowsill?

. . . GEEKS GOT ALL OF THE ATTENTION?

Everyone wants to be popular, especially at school. Some animals love to be popular, too.

Geek Chic

You should never hide how wonderfully clever you are just to fit in at school. In groups of chimps, the dominant one isn't always bigger and tougher than the others. He is cleverer and better at getting his fellow chimps on his side—especially the females.

Popular and Pampered

If you're popular at school, you might get invited to lots of parties or have a load of people trying to talk to you. But if you were like a meerkat, you'd also be stroked and groomed every morning when you got to school.

Sitting Pretty

Dominant velvet worms sit on top of the lower-ranking members of the group. Be thankful that this isn't the way humans treat each other, or else some kids would be in danger of spending their lunchtimes being sat on.

... YOU BUILT A TOWER OF POO?

You'd probably like your bedroom to be a little bubble of happiness, where eagle-eyed parents and nosy brothers and sisters leave you in peace. What's the best way to protect your haven?

Bedroom Watch

A topi (a kind of antelope) produces large piles of poo to mark its territory. It then stands on top of the pile to get a good view of its surroundings. If you did this, not only would you always be able to tell who was sneaking into your bedroom, but also the disgusting smell would deter any unwelcome visitors.

ROTTEN
5
RATING

Butterfly Security

Male comma butterflies spend all day flying around their territory, attacking anything else that flies past, including other insects and even birds. You might need to employ a whole army to protect your bedroom—or even your whole house—this way.

Who Needs a Handshake?

When your cat lovingly rubs his head against your leg, he's marking you as part of his territory with his facial scent glands. What if this were how your best friends greeted you at school every day?

. . . YOU COULD HEADBUTT YOUR RIVALS?

Violence is never the answer, but try telling that to some of the beastly brutes of the animal world, where rivalry can get very nasty.

Strong as an Ox

Male musk oxen fight their rivals with furious headbutting. This is an incredibly bad idea unless you happen to have the massive head-protecting horns of a musk ox. If you don't, then you had better stick with thumb wrestling to settle your differences.

Kick Off

Sometimes male coots (water birds) have kicking contests over a female. If you did this, you'd have the power of flight to help you leap up high and deliver a super-strong kick.

Bloody Bears

By the time polar bears finish their two-week mating season, the males are covered in blood from fighting each other. This might be an attractive look for a polar bear, but it's not a recommended way to impress humans.

SCARY
5
SCORE

. . . GIRLS GOT FIRST PICK AT LUNCH?

Boys don't like to admit it, but sometimes they can be pushed around by girls. Some strange animal behavior, however, takes this one step too far.

Females First

On a boring school day, it's a relief when lunchtime comes around and you get to stuff your face and chill out with your friends. But just imagine if the girls got to eat first. Female spotted hyenas get first pick at every meal a pack enjoys. The boys might be left with only wilted lettuce to eat. It wouldn't really be fair, would it? Unless you're a girl, of course!

Hello, Up There!

If you're very short, you might find it difficult to get noticed. Female echiuroid worms can be a whopping 120 times longer than the male worms. This would be the equivalent of a human woman almost 690 feet (210 meters) tall standing next to an average-size man. That's more than twice as tall as the Statue of Liberty. If human women were this tall, it would be terribly scary to be a man. You'd have to be very careful to keep from getting under a woman's feet—you might accidentally get squished.

HOW HANDY 1

. . . GIRLS DID ALL OF THE WORK?

Sometimes females in the animal world have no choice but to be the ones to take charge because the males of their species are so useless.

Lazy Queens

An ant colony is ruled by a queen who is bigger than all of the worker ants—who are also all females. The worker ants take care of the queen and her babies. That's like your mom employing the help of a hundred of her female friends to take care of everything for her. The only males in an ant colony are called drones. Drone ants don't do any work at all, so they certainly wouldn't be any help.

Hop On

Sometimes female toads have to give their super-lazy partners a piggyback ride to the pond. If this were the only way human men could go to work, the roads would be full of very annoyed women instead of cars.

Mom Hunters

After a female emperor penguin lays an egg, she doesn't sit around waiting for it to hatch. Instead, the dad penguin keeps the egg warm and safe while the mom penguin goes out and hunts for the family. She returns two months later to a hatched baby and a daddy penguin who's probably in need of stretching his legs a bit after all of that sitting.

. . . GIRLS WERE IN CHARGE?

Bossy Ladies

Move over, boys. Let the ladies take control.

- Elephant herds are led by the dominant female. None of the members want to get on the wrong side of her.

- Female birds of prey can be nearly twice as heavy as the males. Now that's really something to squawk about.

- Only female mosquitoes bite humans. Male mosquitoes are vegetarians who get their nutrients from plants and nectars.

- Clownfish live in groups of males, led by one dominant female. Does a male take charge if the female dies? Sure, but he has to change into a female clownfish first.

Super Sniffer

A mother harp seal becomes a super scent detective when looking for her baby in a group of hundreds of other seals on the Arctic ice. Her amazing sense of smell guides her to her little one. Imagine if your mom had to sniff all of the kids at the playground to find you instead of just calling out that it's time to go home. How embarrassing!

. . . *YOU DRESSED UP IN FEATHERS?*

Some male animals really have to look special if they have any hope of impressing the ladies. But their idea of what looks special might be slightly different from yours.

Fashion Tips from a Peacock

Want to look as fabulous as a peacock? Here's how:

1. Grow a shimmering plumage of green and blue feathers, complete with a spectacularly long tail.

2. When you need the "wow" factor, display your tail like a huge, swaying fan.

3. Complete the look with a pretty crest on top of your head.

Singing Star

Female great reed warbler birds only choose companions who can sing very complicated songs. They spend several days listening to and comparing a few different males before picking a lucky winner. It can be hard enough to impress someone, even without having to go through a cringe-worthy talent contest too.

SMART 3 POINTS

Damsel Disguises

Male ruffs (wading birds) can fool other males by looking like females. This way, they can sneak closer to the real females without being beaten up by other males. A smart move—if you don't mind dressing like a girl.

SMART 4 POINTS

. . . YOU USED A PEBBLE TO PROPOSE?

From presents of pebbles to showers of poo, animals can be very giving. Why not take note of these tips?

Present a Pebble

The best gift a male Adélie penguin can give to his mate is a pebble for her nest. So forget a diamond ring—here's how a suitor could propose like a penguin:

1. He must find a great-looking pebble. It shouldn't be too large or have any sharp edges.

2. The pebble must be taken home for a good polish. Then he should decide on the best time and place to surprise his special someone.

3. He should get down on one knee and present his pebble in a romantic way.

4. As soon as his special someone sees how shiny and beautiful the pebble is, she will be over the moon.

Feet Friendly

A male tortoise often bites the feet of a female to show that he likes her. If human males acted in this way, women would never be able to wear flip-flops again!

Poo Propeller

Male hippos like to shower a mixture of pee and poo over female hippos, spinning their tails like propellers to get a good spray. This might be very touching to female hippos, but if you did it, you might want to advise your friends to wear raincoats.

ROTTEN 5 RATING

. . . SOMEONE DRANK YOUR PEE?

It's fun to make new friends, but would you still feel that way if your new buddy tried to drink your pee? Or if he had a giant claw for a hand?

Pee Pals

It can sometimes be difficult to tell if someone wants to hang out with you or not—but not if you're a giraffe. To figure out if a female giraffe wants to hang out with him, a male tastes her pee. If humans did the same, all they'd need to do is take one sneaky sip, and they might be able to save themselves a whole lot of bother.

ROTTEN
3
RATING

Creepy Claws

Having trouble making friends? All you need is a giant claw. One of the male fiddler crab's two claws grows much larger than the other. The male waves his monster claw around and whacks it on the ground to entice females. Human females probably wouldn't appreciate this kind of attention.

Love You and Leaf You

Butterflies don't have great eyesight and may attempt to befriend dead leaves by mistake. If you find yourself accidentally hugging a leaf, you might need a new pair of glasses.

Reader's Digest Books for Young Readers

I Wish I Knew That

This fun and engaging book will give young readers a jump start on everything from art, music, literature, and ancient myths to history, geography, science, and math.

STEVE MARTIN, DR. MIKE GOLDSMITH, AND MARIANNE TAYLOR
978-1-60652-340-7

Killer History

Take a trip through the past and around the globe to discover the most dreadful methods, craziest causes, and unbelievably fascinating facts surrounding the way people died.

CLIVE GIFFORD • 978-1-62145-029-0

Liar! Liar! Pants on Fire!

Sometimes the truth can be so strange that it's hard to believe. With hundreds of incredible true—and false—questions, kids have a great time testing their knowledge, learning fascinating truths, and uncovering lousy lies!

JAN PAYNE • 978-1-60652-476-3

Out of This World

Are you baffled by the Big Bang? Curious about what it's like to walk on the moon? Bursting with intergalactic information, this book gives you everything you need to know about space, from the Earth's atmosphere to the edge of the universe.

CLIVE GIFFORD • 978-1-60652-519-7

Other Titles Available in This Series

Teacher's guides are available at RDTradePublishing.com
Each book is $9.99 hardcover. E-book editions also available.

Reader's Digest books can be purchased through retail and online bookstores. In the United States books are distributed by Penguin Group (USA), Inc. For more information or to order books, call 1-800-788-6262.